PLANNING IN
SUIT CONTRACTS

TEST YOUR BRIDGE TECHNIQUE

PLANNING IN SUIT CONTRACTS

David Bird
Tim Bourke

MASTER POINT PRESS • TORONTO

Master Point Press
331 Douglas Ave.
Toronto, Ontario, Canada
M5M 1H2
(416) 781-0351
Website: http://www.masterpointpress.com
Email: info@masterpointpress.com

National Library of Canada Cataloguing in Publication

Bird, David, 1946-
        Planning in Suit Contracts / David Bird, Tim Bourke

(Test your bridge technique)
ISBN 1-894154-74-6

        1. Contract bridge. I. Bourke, Tim II. Title. III. Series:
Bird, David, 1946-. Test your bridge technique.

GV1282.435.B57212 2004   795.41'52   C2004-902177-X

Editor   ·   Ray Lee
Cover and interior design   Olena S. Sullivan/New Mediatrix

1 2 3 4 5 6 7   09 08 07 06 05 04
Printed in Canada.

INTRODUCTION

This book is designed to accompany *Planning in Suit Contracts*, Book 6 in the *Bridge Technique* series. It will give you the opportunity to practice planning declarer play in situations that involve many of the key techniques relevant to contracts in a trump suit.

While we start out gently, it is only fair to tell you that by the end of this book you will be working hard. To solve the later problems you will need to understand not only how to make a plan but also some fairly advanced cardplay techniques. It will be an exciting journey, though, and the winning lines of play will be clearly explained in the solutions. By acquiring the discipline of always making a plan before you embark on a contract, you will greatly improve your results when you return to a real card table.

PLANNING THE PLAY IN A SUIT CONTRACT

The first step in planning a suit contract is to look at the hand containing the longer trumps, usually declarer's hand, and to count the number of potential losers there. You may not be familiar with this process, so let's see an example. Suppose you have to plan how to play 6♡ on this deal, after West has led the ♠Q:

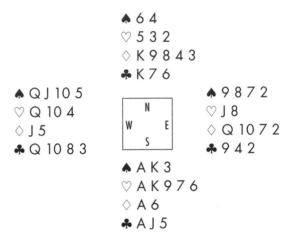

```
            ♠ 6 4
            ♡ 5 3 2
            ◇ K 9 8 4 3
            ♣ K 7 6
♠ Q J 10 5              ♠ 9 8 7 2
♡ Q 10 4       N       ♡ J 8
◇ J 5      W       E   ◇ Q 10 7 2
♣ Q 10 8 3     S       ♣ 9 4 2
            ♠ A K 3
            ♡ A K 9 7 6
            ◇ A 6
            ♣ A J 5
```

You must count the potential losing tricks in the long-trump hand (South). Look at the spades first: the ace and king are certain to score tricks but the ♠3 is a potential loser. In the trump suit (hearts) you have one, two or three possible losers, depending on how the defenders' cards break. In diamonds you have no potential losers. You don't count the ◇6 as a loser because it faces the master ◇K in the dummy. You have only two diamonds in your hand and they are covered by the ace and the king. In clubs you have a potential loser on the third round. You have three clubs in your hand and they are not completely covered by your ace and dummy's king. So, this is the loser situation:

Possible losers in spades:	*1*
Possible losers in hearts:	*3*
Possible losers in diamonds:	*0*
Possible losers in clubs:	*1*

That is a total of five possible losers and you can afford only one loser. The next step in making a plan is to decide which line of play will give you the best chance of reducing your loser-count to one.

There are four main ways of avoiding a potential loser:

> *A suit breaks favorably, and the loser becomes a winner*
> *You take a successful finesse*
> *You ruff a loser in the short trump hand*
> *You discard a loser on a winner in the dummy*

Look at the trump suit on the present deal: you have

♡ 5 3 2

♡ A K 9 7 6

If the suit breaks 3-2 you will have just one loser. If instead it breaks 4-1, you will have two losers. There is nothing much you can do about that, so just hope for the best.

Now look at the spade suit. You can save yourself a loser there by ruffing the third round of spades in dummy (the short-trump hand).

How might you avoid the potential club loser? One possibility is to finesse the ♣J. This relies on luck, however. You would prefer to discard your club loser on dummy's diamonds, if you can set them up.

So this slam deal may allow you to use all four of the main ways to avoid a loser. Let's think how the play will go. You win the spade lead in your hand. You then play the ace and king of trumps, pleased to see a 3-2 break. What will you do next? Ruff the spade loser?

No, because you are hoping to set up the diamonds and a spade ruff will be an important entry to dummy. You play the ace and king of diamonds and ruff a diamond. It makes no difference whether West chooses to overruff with the master ♡Q. Let's assume that he doesn't. You cross to dummy by ruffing your spade loser and ruff another diamond, setting up a long diamond in the dummy. You can then cross to the ♣K and discard your club loser on the established diamond winner. During this process West can take his ♡Q whenever he pleases.

An experienced player would regard this as a straightforward hand to play. That may be the case when you have been playing bridge for many years but you can be sure that a good fraction of players at your local club would have gone down. For a start it was barely possible to make ten tricks unless you paused at the beginning to make a definite plan of action. You then had to arrange the order of the play so that you had sufficient entries to dummy to set up the diamonds when the suit broke 4-2.

Let's look at another deal:

```
                    ♠ K 5 3
                    ♡ K J 8
                    ◇ J 6 5 2
                    ♣ J 7 3
    ♠ Q 9 6 2                      ♠ 10 8 4
    ♡ 7 4              N           ♡ 6 5 3
    ◇ 10 8 7 3    W       E        ◇ Q 9 4
    ♣ K Q 2           S           ♣ A 9 8 6
                    ♠ A J 7
                    ♡ A Q 10 9 2
                    ◇ A K
                    ♣ 10 5 4
```

You bid to 4♡ and West leads the ♣K, the defenders taking three tricks in the suit. How should you plan the remainder of the play when East exits with a low trump?

Your three losers in clubs have been claimed by the defenders already. The only remaining potential loser is in spades. A successful finesse of the ♠J might come to your rescue. Is there any other chance? Yes, if the ◇Q is only twice guarded, you can ruff it out and set up dummy's ◇J for a spade discard. How should the play go?

You win the trump return and draw a second round of trumps, the suit breaking 3-2. You then cash the two diamond honors in your hand and cross to dummy with a third round of trumps. When you ruff a diamond in your hand the queen falls from East. You then return to dummy with the ♠K and discard your spade loser on the established ◇J. If the ◇Q had not fallen in three rounds, you would have fallen back on your second chance — a finesse of the ♠J.

It is nearly always better to combine two chances rather than rely on just one. Here is another example:

```
              ♠ K 4 2
              ♡ K J 4
              ◇ A Q J 7
              ♣ 10 8 6
  ♠ Q 10 8                      ♠ 9 5
  ♡ 9 7 2          N           ♡ 10 8 6 5
  ◇ 10 8 2     W       E       ◇ 9 5 3
  ♣ K J 5 2         S           ♣ Q 9 7 3
              ♠ A J 7 6 3
              ♡ A Q 3
              ◇ K 6 4
              ♣ A 4
```

You reach a small slam in spades and West makes just the lead you did not want to see — a club. East plays the ♣Q and you win with the ace. What is your plan for twelve tricks?

You have one loser in clubs and one or more potential losers in the trump suit. Looking at the trump suit in isolation, the best play to avoid any losers would be to play the king and then finesse the ♠J. You would succeed whenever trumps broke 3-2 and the ♠Q lay with East. In other words, you would succeed on half the 3-2 trump breaks. If you play trumps that way and the finesse loses, however, West will cash a club trick and you will be down one.

A better idea is to combine two chances. You start by playing the king and ace of trumps. This is the second-best play in trumps and will succeed only when trumps break 3-2 and the ♠Q is doubleton (which will happen in two-fifths of the 3-2 breaks). If the queen fails to appear, which is what will happen when the cards lie as in the diagram, you will not yet be dead! You can turn to the diamond suit, hoping that the defender with the last trump has to follow to at least three rounds. You will then be able to discard your club loser on the fourth round of diamonds, making your slam.

So, by taking a slightly inferior line in the trump suit you are able to benefit from a huge second chance: trying to discard your club loser on the diamonds.

We have looked very briefly at how you should set about making a plan as declarer in a suit contract. It is now your turn to step forward and test your own skills. Thirty-six problems await you. Good luck!

Problem 1 ●

♠ K 8 6
♡ A Q J 6
◇ A 8 6
♣ A K 10

◇Q led

♠ A Q J 10 5 3
♡ 7
◇ 7 2
♣ J 9 7 3

WEST	NORTH	EAST	SOUTH
			2♠*
pass	2NT*	pass	3♠*
pass	6♠	all pass	

West leads the ◇Q against your spade slam. How will you plan the play?

Problem 2 ●

♠ 9 7 3
♡ K 8 6 2
◇ J
♣ K Q 10 6 3

♠K led

♠ A 10 8 4
♡ A 9 7 5 3
◇ A K
♣ A 9

WEST	NORTH	EAST	SOUTH
			1♡
pass	3♡	pass	6♡
all pass			

West leads the ♠K against your heart slam. How will you play?

Problem 3

           ♠ A 8 7 5 3 2
           ♡ 3
           ◇ A Q J
           ♣ A 8 4

♣Q led

           ♠ J 6
           ♡ A K 10 9 8 7 2
           ◇ 7
           ♣ 7 3 2

WEST	NORTH	EAST	SOUTH
			3♡
pass	4♡	all pass	

West leads the ♣Q against your heart game. How will you play?

Problem 4

           ♠ Q 2
           ♡ 10 6
           ◇ Q 10 9 8 4
           ♣ A J 10 6

♠A led

           ♠ 9 7 5
           ♡ A K 7 5 3 2
           ◇ A K J
           ♣ 7

WEST	NORTH	EAST	SOUTH
1♠	pass	pass	3♡
pass	4♡	all pass	

West leads the ♠A against your heart game. Realizing that you might wish to ruff a spade in dummy, he switches to the ♡Q. What is your plan?

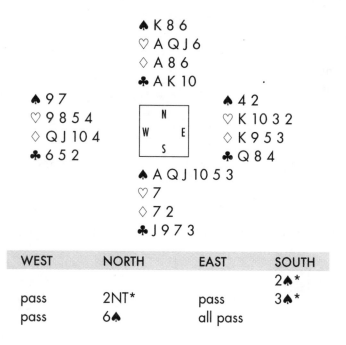

♠ K 8 6
♡ A Q J 6
◇ A 8 6
♣ A K 10

♠ 9 7
♡ 9 8 5 4
◇ Q J 10 4
♣ 6 5 2

♠ 4 2
♡ K 10 3 2
◇ K 9 5 3
♣ Q 8 4

♠ A Q J 10 5 3
♡ 7
◇ 7 2
♣ J 9 7 3

WEST	NORTH	EAST	SOUTH
			2♠*
pass	2NT*	pass	3♠*
pass	6♠	all pass	

Your 3♠ rebid showed a maximum weak two-bid including two of the top three trump honors. West leads the ◇Q against 6♠. Looking at the South hand, you see one diamond loser and one potential further loser (to the queen) in clubs. What chances are there of reducing two losers to one?

Looking at the clubs in isolation, you have the possibility of a successful finesse against the queen. If the ♣Q then fell in three rounds, or trumps broke 2-2 and you could ruff the fourth round of clubs, you would avoid any loser in the suit. The only chance of avoiding a diamond loser is to take a heart finesse, or a ruffing heart finesse, hoping to set up a diamond discard on the extra heart trick that you establish. What is the best way of combining these chances?

Suppose you draw trumps and play a heart to the queen. The sun will shine if the finesse wins. If it loses, East will cash a diamond for down one. A better idea, after drawing trumps, is to play the $\heartsuit$A and $\heartsuit$Q, intending to throw a diamond. If East produces the $\heartsuit$K, you will ruff and cross to a top club to throw a diamond on the $\heartsuit$J. You can then afford to lose a club trick. If instead the ruffing finesse loses to West's king, you will fall back on a finesse against the $\clubsuit$Q. Your fourth club can then be thrown on the $\heartsuit$J, if necessary.

We have decided on the main plan, then: you wll take a ruffing finesse in hearts, falling back on the club finesse if it fails. Good cardplayers like to give themselves n extra edge wherever possible. On this deal, for example, you should play the $\heartsuit$A and ruff the $\heartsuit$6 before taking a rufifng finesse in the suit. By doing so, you will avoid going down when West started with $\heartsuit$K-x. Similarly, it is good technique to cash the $\clubsuit$A before taking the club finesse; int his way you avoid losing to a singleton $\clubsuit$Q with East.

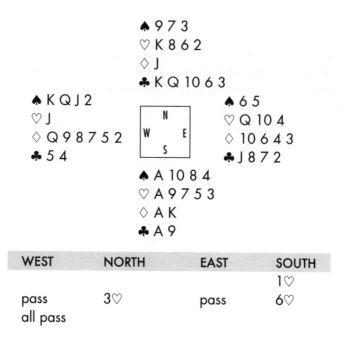

♠ 9 7 3
♡ K 8 6 2
◇ J
♣ K Q 10 6 3

♠ K Q J 2
♡ J
◇ Q 9 8 7 5 2
♣ 5 4

♠ 6 5
♡ Q 10 4
◇ 10 6 4 3
♣ J 8 7 2

♠ A 10 8 4
♡ A 9 7 5 3
◇ A K
♣ A 9

WEST	NORTH	EAST	SOUTH
			1♡
pass	3♡	pass	6♡
all pass			

How will you play the small slam in hearts when West leads the ♠K? If trumps break 2-2, all will be easy. What can you do if the trumps are 3-1? You will then need to discard all three spade losers on dummy's clubs before the defender with the master trump can ruff in and cash a spade or two. If you think about it, you will realize that the defender with the third trump will need to hold four clubs. He will then follow to four rounds of clubs, as you pitch two spades. On the fifth round you will pitch your last spade, not caring if he ruffs with his master trump.

The clubs are not solid, though. You are missing the ♣J. When clubs do break 4-2 (as you must hope in the case of a 3-1 trump break), the odds are 2-to-1 that the ♣J will lie in the four-card holding. So, win the spade lead and play the ace and king of trumps.

Here East turns up with a trump trick, so it is best to play him for ♣Jxxx. You finesse the ♣9 successfully and cash the ♣A. You then play the ◇A and reach dummy by ruffing the ◇K. Two more club winners allow you to throw two spades, East following all the while. Finally you lead dummy's fifth club and throw your last spade. Slam bid, slam made.

If instead West had turned up with three trumps, you would have finessed him for ♣Jxxx. After two rounds of trumps you would have crossed to the ♣A and led the ♣9, overtaking with dummy's ♣10.

.

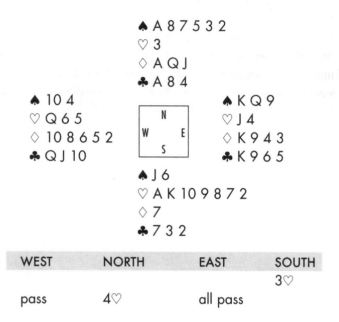

♠ A 8 7 5 3 2
♡ 3
◇ A Q J
♣ A 8 4

♠ 10 4
♡ Q 6 5
◇ 10 8 6 5 2
♣ Q J 10

♠ K Q 9
♡ J 4
◇ K 9 4 3
♣ K 9 6 5

♠ J 6
♡ A K 10 9 8 7 2
◇ 7
♣ 7 3 2

WEST	NORTH	EAST	SOUTH
			3♡
pass	4♡	all pass	

West leads the ♣Q against your heart game and you pause to make a plan. You have two potential losers in clubs, a loser in spades and (you must hope) just one loser in the trump suit. How can you reduce the total from four losers to three?

One possibility is a straightforward finesse of the ◇Q. If that wins, you will be able to discard a loser on the diamond ace. If the diamond finesse loses, though, you will go down. The defenders will grab two club tricks and an eventual trump loser will defeat you.

A better idea is a ruffing finesse in diamonds. You win the club lead and play the two top trumps, pleased to see a 3-2 break. You then cross to the ◇A and lead the ◇Q. If East covers, you will ruff and concede a third round of trumps. Eventually you will cross to the ♠A and discard your spade loser on the established ◇J. If instead East follows low when you lead the $\diamond$Q, you will discard a club. You don't mind if West wins with the $\diamond$K because the defenders will score only one diamond trick, one club trick and one trump. When you regain the lead you will again be able to throw your spade loser on the established $\diamond$J.

With the sort of holding that you have here in diamonds, a ruffing finesse is often better than a straightforward finesse. That's because you can get one loser away before the defenders gain the lead.

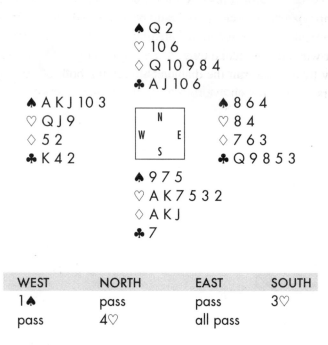

♠ Q 2
♡ 10 6
◇ Q 10 9 8 4
♣ A J 10 6

♠ A K J 10 3
♡ Q J 9
◇ 5 2
♣ K 4 2

N
W   E
S

♠ 8 6 4
♡ 8 4
◇ 7 6 3
♣ Q 9 8 5 3

♠ 9 7 5
♡ A K 7 5 3 2
◇ A K J
♣ 7

WEST	NORTH	EAST	SOUTH
1♠	pass	pass	3♡
pass	4♡	all pass	

West leads the ♠A against your heart game and switches to the
queen of trumps. What is your plan to make the contract?

You have three potential losers in spades and (you must hope)
only one further loser in trumps. Since there is no distribution that
will allow you to avoid the loser in the trump suit, you must find a
way to dispose of your third spade. The trump switch has killed
any hopes you might have had of ruffing the third spade. If you
win the trump switch and play another spade, preparing for a ruff,
West will win and play another round of trumps. Your only hope
then will be that the defender with the last trump also holds three
diamonds. In that case you could cash three diamonds without
suffering a ruff and throw your last spade on the fourth round of

diamonds. When the cards lie as the diagram, West would ruff the third diamond and cash a spade for down one.

The solution is to duck West's ♡Q switch! You have to lose a trump trick anyway and it makes good sense to do so at a moment when the defenders cannot do you any damage. West is powerless after winning the second trick. If he plays another trump, you will draw trumps and run the diamonds, throwing both of your spade losers and scoring an overtrick.

Problem 5

```
             ♠ 9 4
             ♡ J 8 3
             ◇ A 7 6 5 2
             ♣ A 10 2
♣K led
             ♠ A K 6 2
             ♡ A K 6 5 4 2
             ◇ Q
             ♣ 8 5
```

WEST	NORTH	EAST	SOUTH
1♠	pass	pass	3♡
pass	4♡	all pass	

West leads the ♣K against your comfortable-looking game in hearts. How will you play the contract for maximum safety?

Problem 6

```
             ♠ 8 5 3 2
             ♡ Q 10 9 4
             ◇ 6 2
             ♣ A 7 3
◇Q led
             ♠ A K Q J 10 7
             ♡ A
             ◇ A K 9
             ♣ J 10 4
```

WEST	NORTH	EAST	SOUTH
			2♣
pass	2◇	pass	2♠
pass	3♠	pass	4◇
pass	5♣	pass	6♠
all pass			

West leads the ◇Q against 6♠. What is your plan?

Problem 7

♠ K 8 5
♡ K 6 2
◇ K 10 2
♣ K 7 6 4

♣Q led

♠ A Q J 10 6
♡ A Q 8 7 4
◇ A 5
♣ 2

WEST	NORTH	EAST	SOUTH
	1♣	pass	1♠
pass	1NT	pass	3♡
pass	3♠	pass	6♠
all pass			

West leads the ♣Q against your spade slam. How will you play?

Problem 8

♠ J 6
♡ A K 6 4 3
◇ K 8 7 4
♣ J 10

♣K led

♠ A Q 10 7 3 2
♡ 8 5
◇ A 3
♣ 8 7 5

WEST	NORTH	EAST	SOUTH
			1♠
2♣	2♡	pass	2♠
pass	3◇	pass	3♠
pass	4♠	all pass	

West cashes two top clubs, East playing the ♣9 and the ♣2. West continues with the ♣Q at Trick 3. What is your plan?

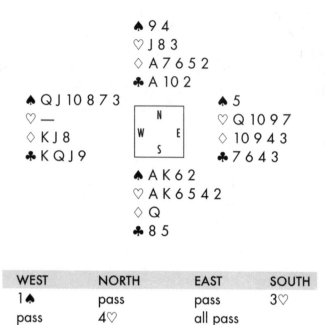

| ♠ 9 4 |
| ♡ J 8 3 |
| ◇ A 7 6 5 2 |
| ♣ A 10 2 |

♠ Q J 10 8 7 3
♡ —
◇ K J 8
♣ K Q J 9

♠ 5
♡ Q 10 9 7
◇ 10 9 4 3
♣ 7 6 4 3

♠ A K 6 2
♡ A K 6 5 4 2
◇ Q
♣ 8 5

WEST	NORTH	EAST	SOUTH
1♠	pass	pass	3♡
pass	4♡	all pass	

West leads the ♣K against your heart game. Although there is no direct benefit on this deal, it is sound technique to win the second club rather than the first, to restrict the defenders' communications.

How many potential losers do you have in the South hand? Two in spades, one in clubs and zero-to-two in the trump suit, depending on how the defenders' cards lie. Since there are nowhere near enough entries to set up dummy's diamonds, you must aim to ruff two spades. West's opening 1♠ bid tells you that East will overruff but this may be at the expense of a natural trump trick or two.

What is the main risk to the contract? If East has a singleton spade, you must be careful not to give him a chance to ruff one of your spade honors. So, win the second club and lead a spade towards your hand. East follows and the spade ace wins. Return to dummy with the $\diamond$A and lead a second spade towards your hand. East has no spades left but since you are leading towards your remaining honor, he is powerless. Ruffing thin air with a natural trump trick would not make much sense, so he discards a club. You win with the spade king and ruff a spade with the jack. East over-ruffs with the queen but he cannot do you any damage. You ruff his minor-suit return, play the ace of trumps (West showing out) and ruff your last spade in the dummy. Once again East overruffs but your contract is secure.

Noet that it would be poor play to 'test the trumps' by playing the $\heartsuit$A before ruffing any spades. Eas would then overruff the second round of spades and remove dummy's last trump. Deprived of your second spade ruff, you would lose one spade, two trumps and a club, going one down.

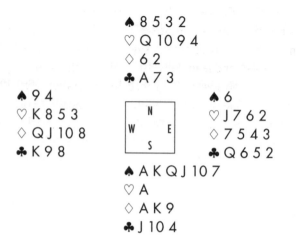

♠ 8 5 3 2
♡ Q 10 9 4
◇ 6 2
♣ A 7 3

♠ 9 4
♡ K 8 5 3
◇ Q J 10 8
♣ K 9 8

♠ 6
♡ J 7 6 2
◇ 7 5 4 3
♣ Q 6 5 2

♠ A K Q J 10 7
♡ A
◇ A K 9
♣ J 10 4

WEST	NORTH	EAST	SOUTH
			2♣
pass	2◇	pass	2♠
pass	3♠	pass	4◇
pass	5♣	pass	6♠
all pass			

West leads the ◇Q against 6♠. You have three potential losers in the long-trump (South) hand — one diamond and two clubs. The diamond loser can easily be ruffed. How can you avoid one of the club losers?

If you held the ♣9, as well as the ♣J and ♣10, you could take two finesses in clubs. Since the ♣9 is held by the defenders, prospects in the club suit alone are very poor. You should look to dummy's heart suit for your salvation, planning to take two ruffing finesses through East.

Win the diamond lead with the ace and draw trumps in two rounds. After cashing the ♡A, you play your remaining diamond honor and reach dummy with a diamond ruff. Now comes the first of the two ruffing finesses in hearts. You lead the ♡Q and, when East does not produce the ♡K, discard a club loser from your hand. West wins with the ♡K and, let's say, switches to a club. You rise with dummy's ♣A and lead the ♡10. If East fails to cover, you will throw your last club loser. If instead he covers with the ♡J, you must be careful! You must ruff with a trump honor. You can then return to dummy by overtaking the ♠7 with the ♠8, to discard your last club on the established ♡9.

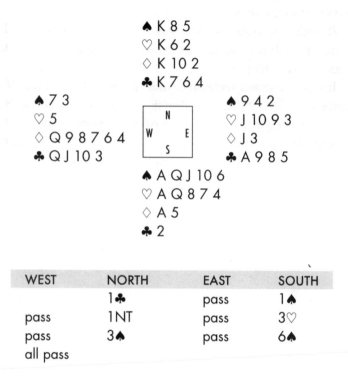

♠ K 8 5
♡ K 6 2
◇ K 10 2
♣ K 7 6 4

♠ 7 3
♡ 5
◇ Q 9 8 7 6 4
♣ Q J 10 3

♠ 9 4 2
♡ J 10 9 3
◇ J 3
♣ A 9 8 5

♠ A Q J 10 6
♡ A Q 8 7 4
◇ A 5
♣ 2

WEST	NORTH	EAST	SOUTH
	1♣	pass	1♠
pass	1NT	pass	3♡
pass	3♠	pass	6♠
all pass			

You don't regard that North hand as an opening bid? No, indeed – you may want to talk to partner about this later! Anyway, West leads the ♣Q against your small slam in spades. How will you play the contract?

There is little point in playing dummy's ♣K on the opening lead, although it does not really matter on this deal. West's club queen wins the first trick and he plays another club, which you ruff. When you play two rounds of trumps, both defenders follow. It may now seem that all depends on a 3-2 heart break. However, you can give yourself a considerable extra chance by testing the hearts before drawing the last trump. When you play the king and ace of hearts,

West shows out but cannot ruff. You continue with the queen of hearts and ruff the fourth round of hearts in the dummy. You can then return to your hand with the ◇A and draw the last trump. It's time to claim the slam!

If both defenders had followed to two hearts you would, of course, have drawn the last trump before running the remaining tricks.

It's an important technique to draw some, but not all, of the trumps before attempting a ruff. By doing so, you can improve your chances in a quite different situation — when there is a risk of an overruff. The defender who is out of the suit that you are ruffing may then have no trump left with which to overruff.

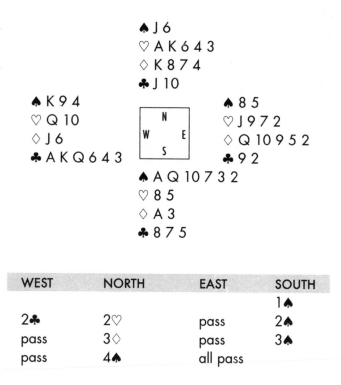

♠ J 6
♡ A K 6 4 3
◇ K 8 7 4
♣ J 10

♠ K 9 4
♡ Q 10
◇ J 6
♣ A K Q 6 4 3

♠ 8 5
♡ J 9 7 2
◇ Q 10 9 5 2
♣ 9 2

♠ A Q 10 7 3 2
♡ 8 5
◇ A 3
♣ 8 7 5

WEST	NORTH	EAST	SOUTH
			1♠
2♣	2♡	pass	2♠
pass	3◇	pass	3♠
pass	4♠	all pass	

West cashes two top clubs against your spade game, East playing the ♣9 and the ♣2. West continues with the ♣Q at Trick 3. What is your plan for the contract?

Ruffing with the ♠6 is no good. East will overruff with the ♠8 and you will lose a subsequent trump trick to West's king. Instead you should ruff with the ♠J, which East cannot overruff. What now?

There are two good reasons not to take a trump finesse. The first is that East is unlikely to hold the ♠K when he failed to overruff dummy's ♠J. The second is that if you do take a losing trump finesse, West will lead a fourth round of clubs. East will ruff with the ♠8, forcing you to overruff with the ♠10, and that will promote his partner's ♠9. Down one!

To avoid this outcome, you should continue with the ace and queen of trumps. West wins with the ♠K but there is only one trump outstanding and the defenders have no way in which to promote it. When you regain the lead, you will draw the last trump and claim the contract.

Problem 9

♠ Q J 6
♡ Q 10 9
◇ A 6
♣ J 7 6 4 2

◇K led

♠ 8 4 3
♡ A K J 5 4 3
◇ 7 4
♣ A K

WEST	NORTH	EAST	SOUTH
			1♡
pass	2♣	pass	3♡
pass	4♡	all pass	

West leads the ◇K against your heart game. Plan the play.

Problem 10

♠ 3
♡ 10 6 4 3
◇ K 9 7 5 4
♣ 6 4 2

♡7 led

♠ A 9 8 6 2
♡ A K Q J 9 5
◇ A
♣ A

WEST	NORTH	EAST	SOUTH
			2♣
pass	2◇	pass	2♡
pass	3♠*	pass	4NT
pass	5♣*	pass	5NT
pass	6◇*	pass	7♡
all pass			

West leads the ♡7 against your grand slam. How will you play?

Problem 11

♠ A J 10 4 2
♡ A Q
◇ 10 7 4
♣ A Q J

♡J led

♠ 8
♡ K 5
◇ A 8 5 2
♣ K 10 9 8 5 2

WEST	NORTH	EAST	SOUTH
			1♣
pass	1♠	pass	2♣
pass	2♡	pass	2NT
pass	4♣	pass	4◇
pass	6♣	all pass	

How will you play when West leads the ♡J?

Problem 12

♠ K 8 2
♡ A K 9
◇ A K 8 5 3 2
♣ 7

♠3 led

♠ A Q J 10 9 6
♡ —
◇ 9 4
♣ A 8 5 4 2

WEST	NORTH	EAST	SOUTH
	1◇	pass	1♠
pass	3◇	pass	3♠
pass	4NT	pass	5♠*
pass	7♠	all pass	

West leads a trump against 7♠. How will you play?

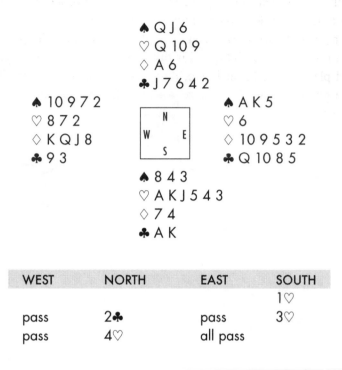

♠ Q J 6
♡ Q 10 9
◇ A 6
♣ J 7 6 4 2

♠ 10 9 7 2
♡ 8 7 2
◇ K Q J 8
♣ 9 3

N
W E
S

♠ A K 5
♡ 6
◇ 10 9 5 3 2
♣ Q 10 8 5

♠ 8 4 3
♡ A K J 5 4 3
◇ 7 4
♣ A K

WEST	NORTH	EAST	SOUTH
			1♡
pass	2♣	pass	3♡
pass	4♡	all pass	

West leads the ◇K against your heart game. You have three potential losers in spades and one in diamonds, giving you a total of four.
What is the best prospect of reducing this number to three?

One simple possibility is to draw trumps and lead twice towards
dummy's spade honors. Provided West has at least one of the missing spade honors, you will set up a spade trick in dummy and make
the contract. West would surely have led a spade if he held both the
ace and king, so the chance of him holding one of the spade honors
is only 2 in 3, about 66%.

A better chance is to set up dummy's club suit but to do this you
will have to leave dummy's trump entries intact. After winning the
diamond lead with the ace, you cash the ace and king of clubs. Both

defenders follow, you are pleased to see, and you cross to dummy with a trump to the nine. (If trumps are 4-0, you will have to abandon the plan to set up the clubs, draw trumps and lead twice towards the spades.) When both defenders follow, you ruff a club high, West showing out. You then return to dummy with the ♡10 and ruff another club high. Finally you cross to the trump queen and play the established club, throwing the diamond loser. This line gives you an 77% chance, much better than leading towards the spades twice.

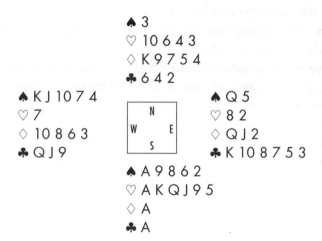

```
                    ♠ 3
                    ♡ 10 6 4 3
                    ◇ K 9 7 5 4
                    ♣ 6 4 2
♠ K J 10 7 4                        ♠ Q 5
♡ 7              ┌──────────┐       ♡ 8 2
◇ 10 8 6 3      │    N     │       ◇ Q J 2
♣ Q J 9         │ W     E  │       ♣ K 10 8 7 5 3
                │    S     │
                └──────────┘
                    ♠ A 9 8 6 2
                    ♡ A K Q J 9 5
                    ◇ A
                    ♣ A
```

WEST	NORTH	EAST	SOUTH
			2♣
pass	2◇	pass	2♡
pass	3♠*	pass	4NT
pass	5♣*	pass	5NT
pass	6◇*	pass	7♡
all pass			

North's 3♠ is a splinter bid, agreeing hearts and showing at most one
spade. When North shows one king you bid 7♡. You win the trump
lead in your hand. You must make some plan for the four losing
spades. If the suit breaks 4-3, you can ruff two spades with low
trumps and the fourth round with the ♡10. This plan will fail if East
holds only two spades and the last trump. He will overruff on the
third round of spades.

Another chance is that diamonds will break 4-3, providing a second spade discard. In that case you will be able to draw trumps before ruffing the third round of spades.

By timing the play well, you can combine these two chances. Win the trump lead and cash the ◇A and the ♠A. You then ruff a spade low and play dummy's ◇K, discarding a spade. The next move is to ruff a diamond with a high trump. If diamonds break 5-2, you will have only one discard and must risk ruffing the next spade with the ♡6. When the cards lie as in the diagram, both defenders will follow to the third round of diamonds. You will therefore play a trump to the ten, drawing the last trump. You can then ruff the diamonds good and re-enter dummy with a spade ruff to enjoy a discard on the thirteenth diamond.

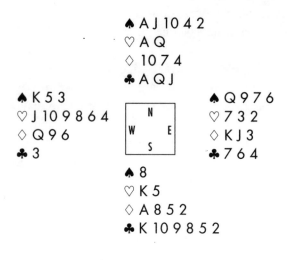

WEST	NORTH	EAST	SOUTH
			1♣
pass	1♠	pass	2♣
pass	2♡	pass	2NT
pass	4♣	pass	4♢
pass	6♣	all pass	

You open light on the South cards and reach a borderline slam. How will you justify partner's faith when West leads the ♡J?

Looking at the losers in the long-trump hand, you see three in the diamond suit. One possible line is an elimination play. If trumps are 2-2, you might be able to eliminate the major suits and then play ace and another diamond. If the defender who won the trick held no more diamonds, he would have to give you a ruff-and-discard. This is a remote prospect, however, because a skillful defender with ♢Kx would unblock the king under your ace, allowing his partner to win the second round of the suit.

A better idea is to set up two extra spade winners in dummy and the best way of attempting this is to finesse on the first round of spades. Win the heart lead with the king and play a spade to the jack and queen. Win the heart return, cash the ♠A, discardig a diamond loser. Now ruff a spade with a high trump. When West's ♠K falls on this trick, you have your slam. You can draw trumps and discard two more diamonds on the ♠104.

This line will succeed also when West holds ♠K-Q-x-x or either defender holds ♠K-Q-x or ♠K-Q doubleton.

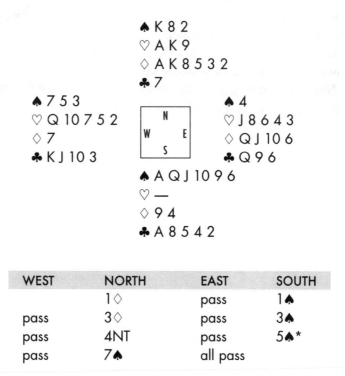

♠ K 8 2
♡ A K 9
◇ A K 8 5 3 2
♣ 7

♠ 7 5 3
♡ Q 10 7 5 2
◇ 7
♣ K J 10 3

♠ 4
♡ J 8 6 4 3
◇ Q J 10 6
♣ Q 9 6

♠ A Q J 10 9 6
♡ —
◇ 9 4
♣ A 8 5 4 2

WEST	NORTH	EAST	SOUTH
	1◇	pass	1♠
pass	3◇	pass	3♠
pass	4NT	pass	5♠*
pass	7♠	all pass	

West leads a trump against your grand slam in spades. To make the contract you must dispose of all four club losers. Suppose your plan is to ruff one club, discard two clubs on dummy's ♡AK, return to your hand with a heart ruff and ruff your last club. Dummy will have only diamonds left. Now you will need diamonds to break 3-2: on the layout above, for example, when you try to return to your hand with a diamond ruff, West will ruff the second diamond to beat you. What else can you try?

You can establish dummy's diamond suit. This will also be an easy task if diamonds break 3-2, so you should direct your attention to countering a 4-1 diamond break. Win the trump lead with the ♠9, retaining your ♠6, and cross to the ♢A. Discard a diamond on the heart ace and ruff a diamond high. Your precautions are shown to be worthwhile when West discards on the second round of diamonds. You lead the ♠6 to dummy's ♠8 and ruff another diamond high, setting up the suit. A trump to dummy's king draws West's last trump and you can now play three good diamonds and the ♡K, throwing away all four of your club losers.

Note that you needed to 'draw trumps, ending in the dummy'. A club ruff at any stage would have been fatal.

Problem 13

                              ♠ J 8 5 3 2
                              ♡ A 4 2
                              ◇ K 4 3
                              ♣ 6 4

    ♠K led

                              ♠ —
                              ♡ J
                              ◇ A Q 8 7 6 5
                              ♣ A K J 8 7 3

WEST	NORTH	EAST	SOUTH
			1◇
dbl	1♠	pass	3♣
pass	3◇	pass	4♣
pass	4♡	pass	6♣
pass	6◇	all pass	

West leads the ♠K; how will you play? (Trumps are not 4-0.)

Problem 14

                              ♠ Q 4 2
                              ♡ A J 3
                              ◇ A J 6 5 4
                              ♣ K 6

    ♣J led

                              ♠ A K J 10 8 3
                              ♡ K 7
                              ◇ K 9 7
                              ♣ Q 8

WEST	NORTH	EAST	SOUTH
			1♠
pass	2◇	pass	3♠
pass	4NT	pass	5♡*
pass	6♠	all pass	

How should you play the contract on the lead of the ♣J?

Problem 15

```
                    ♠ 7 3
                    ♡ 7 5 3 2
                    ◇ 6 4 3
                    ♣ K 10 9 7
♠ 10 led
                    ♠ A K
                    ♡ A K Q J 10 8
                    ◇ A Q 5
                    ♣ A Q
```

WEST	NORTH	EAST	SOUTH
			2♣
pass	2◇	pass	2♡
pass	3♡	pass	4NT
pass	5♣*	pass	5NT
pass	6◇*	pass	6♡
all pass			

West leads the ♠10 against your slam. How will you play?

Problem 16

```
                    ♠ A 7 6
                    ♡ K 7 5
                    ◇ A 9 6
                    ♣ A 8 5 3
♡ 10 led
                    ♠ Q J 10 9 5 4 2
                    ♡ 9 3
                    ◇ K 8 5
                    ♣ J
```

WEST	NORTH	EAST	SOUTH
	1NT	2♡	4♠
all pass			

West wins the first trick with the ♡10 and continues with a heart to East's jack. How will you play when the ♡A is led to Trick 3?

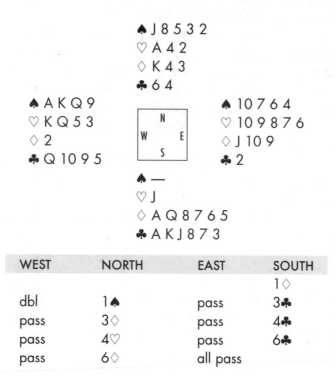

♠ J 8 5 3 2
♡ A 4 2
◇ K 4 3
♣ 6 4

♠ A K Q 9
♡ K Q 5 3
◇ 2
♣ Q 10 9 5

♠ 10 7 6 4
♡ 10 9 8 7 6
◇ J 10 9
♣ 2

♠ —
♡ J
◇ A Q 8 7 6 5
♣ A K J 8 7 3

WEST	NORTH	EAST	SOUTH
			1◇
dbl	1♠	pass	3♣
pass	3◇	pass	4♣
pass	4♡	pass	6♣
pass	6◇	all pass	

West leads the ♠K against your diamond slam. You ruff in your hand and play the ace of trumps, both defenders following. You must now look for a line that will succeed against a 4-1 club break. West is more likely to hold four clubs than East, because he made a take-out double of 1◇.

Cash the club ace, both defenders following. You should now aim to lead the second round of clubs towards your hand, so that if East has only one club he will not be able to ruff your ♣K. You cross to dummy with the ♡A and lead a club towards your hand. If East chooses to ruff a low club, you can easily make the contract by ruffing a club with the king. Let's assume that he discards a heart instead. You win with the club king and lead a third round of clubs. If you ruff this with a low trump, you will go down. East will overruff and return a trump. With no trumps left in dummy, you will be saddled with a further loser in clubs.

To avoid this outcome, you should ruff the third round of clubs with the king. What next? Drawing a second round of trumps is no good because you would then lose a trump trick and a club trick. No, you must reach your hand with a heart ruff and ruff a fourth round of clubs with dummy's last trump, the $\diamond$4. Whether or not East chooses to overruff, you will lose only one trick (a trump trick) and make the slam.

What would have happened if East had followed suit on the second round of clubs? Is it better to finesse the jack or rise with the king? If you rise with the king, you will go down only when West can ruff and then return a trump (to prevent two further ruffs on the table). That would require him to be 3-1 in diamonds and clubs, an unlikely shape after his takeout double of 1$\diamond$. The alternative play of finessing the ♣J is much more likely to result in failure. If the finesse loses to an initial ♣Qxx, West can return a third round of clubs and you would have to ruff high, with dummy's $\diamond$K. You would then go down whenever West was 1-3 in diamonds and clubs, a much more likely shape.

So, if East follows to the second round of clubs you should rise with the ♣K. If West follows suit, the contract is guaranteed. You will lead a third club, ruffing with the $\diamond$K if West follows suit. The most you can lose is one trump trick.

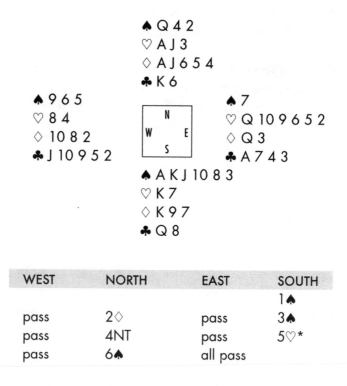

	♠ Q 4 2
	♡ A J 3
	◇ A J 6 5 4
	♣ K 6

WEST	NORTH	EAST	SOUTH
			1♠
pass	2◇	pass	3♠
pass	4NT	pass	5♡*
pass	6♠	all pass	

West leads the ♣J against your small slam in spades. How should you play the contract?

You should play low from dummy. If East fails to play the ♣A, draw two rounds of trumps and throw East in with a club, forcing him to lead a red suit or give you a ruff-and-discard. Suppose instead that East spots the danger of playing low and takes his ♣A at Trick 1. How will you continue when he returns another club?

After drawing trumps, you must dispose of the potential loser in diamonds. What is the best chance of doing this? One possibility is to finesse the ◇J. Another chance is to finesse of the ♡J, setting up a diamond discard on the third round of hearts. The trouble is that you would have to guess which finesse to take first. If your chosen finesse lost, you would be down before you had the chance to take the other finesse.

In situations like this, you should aim to combine two chances. You do this by playing for the drop in one suit, falling back on a finesse in the other suit if necessary. Here you have eight diamonds and only five hearts, so the diamond suit offers the best chance of dropping the missing queen. You play the ◇AK. If the ◇Q does not fall in two rounds, return to your hand with the ♡K and finesse dummy's ♡J.

If you have read the companion book in this series, *The Simple Squeeze*, you will probably realize that you may have other options on this deal in the end position. If you run all your trumps before makin a play in hearts, you will eventually arrve at this ending:

Depending on what has happened in the play so far, you may know whch opponent holds the ◇Q. If the same player also holds the ♡Q, he will have been squeezed. Indeed, if East holds both red queens, you will have made the hand even when both finesses would have lost!

```
                        ♠ 7 3
                        ♡ 7 5 3 2
                        ◇ 6 4 3
                        ♣ K 10 9 7
        ♠ 10 9 8 6 4                        ♠ Q J 5 2
        ♡ —              ┌─────────┐        ♡ 9 6 4
        ◇ K 10 8 2       │    N    │        ◇ J 9 7
        ♣ J 8 3 2        │  W   E  │        ♣ 7 6 5
                         │    S    │
                         └─────────┘
                        ♠ A K
                        ♡ A K Q J 10 8
                        ◇ A Q 5
                        ♣ A Q
```

WEST	NORTH	EAST	SOUTH
			2♣
pass	2◇	pass	2♡
pass	3♡	pass	4NT
pass	5♣*	pass	5NT
pass	6◇*	pass	6♡
all pass			

Once hearts were agreed as trumps, South was willing to play in a grand slam if North held both the minor-suit kings. In the methods being played, 5NT asked how many kings partner held. The 6◇ response revealed only one king in the North hand and the bidding came to a halt in 6♠. How do you play this contract when West leads the ♠10?

The loser position in the long-trump (South) hand is a simple one. You have two potential diamond losers and must somehow avoid one of them. One obvious line is to win the lead, draw trumps, cash the ♣A, reach dummy by overtaking the ♣Q and (unless the ♣J has fallen doubleton) take a diamond finesse. That line is a little over 50%. Is there anything better?

Indeed there is! You should win the spade lead and draw trumps in three rounds. You then cash your other spade winner, eliminating that suit. After cashing the ♣A, you overtake the ♣Q with the ♣K and survey this end position:

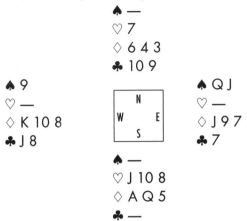

Instead of banking everything on a diamond finesse, you should now lead the ♣10 and throw the ◊5 from your hand. As the cards lie, West will win with the ♣J and will have to give you a trick with his return. A diamond will be into the ace-queen tenace and a club would revive dummy's ♣9, allowing you to discard the ◊Q. West cannot play a spade, of course, since this would concede a ruff-and-discard. You would ruff in the dummy and discard the ◊Q.

What if East had produced the ♣J on the third round? You would still discard a diamond. Since a black-suit return from East would give you the contract, he would have to switch to a diamond. You would then be able to finesse the diamond queen.

You see how much better this line is, compared with simply taking the diamond finesse? You make the contract when East holds the ◊K or when West holds the ♣J. You get two chances instead of one. (Three instead of two, if you include the small one of the ♣J dropping doubleton!)

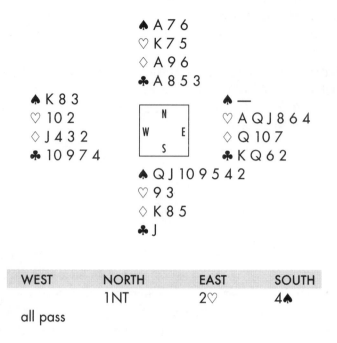

♠ A 7 6
♡ K 7 5
◇ A 9 6
♣ A 8 5 3

♠ K 8 3
♡ 10 2
◇ J 4 3 2
♣ 10 9 7 4

♠ —
♡ A Q J 8 6 4
◇ Q 10 7
♣ K Q 6 2

♠ Q J 10 9 5 4 2
♡ 9 3
◇ K 8 5
♣ J

WEST	NORTH	EAST	SOUTH
	1NT	2♡	4♠

all pass

With a seven-card suit you decide to attempt game, facing your partner's strong 1NT. West leads the ♡10, which wins the first trick, and continues with a second heart to East's ♡J. East then continues with the ace of hearts. How should you play?

You have a certain third loser in diamonds and cannot afford to lose a trump trick as well. You know that West started with only two hearts. Apart from East's overcall, which suggests a six-card suit, West led the ♡10 and you can see the ♡9. Suppose you ruff the third heart with the ♠9. When the cards lie as in the diagram, West will overruff with the king and you will eventually lose a diamond trick for down one. Even if West had been unable to over-ruff the ♠9 you would not be very well placed. Knowing that East must hold the ♠K, you would have to play for that card to drop singleton, which is not a good chance.

The best line of play is to discard your diamond loser on the third round of hearts and then to rely on finessing West for the ♠K. A fourth heart from East would be ineffective because you would ruff with the ♠9 in the South hand, not minding if this was over-ruffed in turn by West's king and dummy's ace. East will probably switch to the ♣K at Trick 4. You win with the ace and ruff a club to reach your hand. You can then pick up the trump suit with a finesse and claim the balance.

Problem 17 ·

                        ♠ K 4
                        ♡ J 10 9 5 3
                        ◇ K 7 4
                        ♣ K 5 3

    ♠Q led

                        ♠ A 6 5 3
                        ♡ K Q 8 6
                        ◇ J 5
                        ♣ A J 6

WEST	NORTH	EAST	SOUTH
			1NT
pass	2◇*	pass	2♡
pass	3NT	pass	4♡
all pass			

West leads the ♠Q against 4♡. What is your plan?

Problem 18 ·

                        ♠ Q 9 3
                        ♡ 10 3 2
                        ◇ 10 7
                        ♣ A 9 8 5 3

    ♡K led

                        ♠ A K J 10 7 4
                        ♡ A 8 6 4
                        ◇ A 4
                        ♣ 6

WEST	NORTH	EAST	SOUTH
			1♠
pass	2♠	pass	4♠
all pass			

West leads the ♡K. What is your plan to safeguard the contract?

Problem 19

♠ J 10 8 7
♡ A K 7 5 2
◇ 7 4
♣ A 8

♡Q led

♠ A K Q 9 3
♡ 3
◇ A K 10 6 2
♣ K 2

WEST	NORTH	EAST	SOUTH
	1♡	pass	1♠
pass	2♠	pass	4NT
pass	5♡*	pass	7♠
all pass			

West leads the ♡Q against your grand slam. Plan the play.

Problem 20

♠ 8
♡ 8 6 2
◇ 8 7 3 2
♣ 9 8 7 4 2

♡K led

♠ A K Q J 6
♡ 7
◇ A J 10
♣ K Q J 6

WEST	NORTH	EAST	SOUTH
1♡	pass	2♡	dbl
3♡	pass	pass	4♠
all pass			

West leads the ♡AK against your spade game. How will you play?

```
                    ♠ K 4
                    ♡ J 10 9 5 3
                    ◇ K 7 4
                    ♣ K 5 3
  ♠ Q J 10 8 2                      ♠ 9 7
  ♡ 4 2          ┌─────────┐        ♡ A 7
  ◇ 9 8 3        │    N    │        ◇ A Q 10 6 2
  ♣ Q 7 2        │ W     E │        ♣ 10 9 8 4
                 │    S    │
                 └─────────┘
                    ♠ A 6 5 3
                    ♡ K Q 8 6
                    ◇ J 5
                    ♣ A J 6
```

WEST	NORTH	EAST	SOUTH
			1NT
pass	2◇*	pass	2♡
pass	3NT	pass	4♡
all pass			

West leads the ♠Q against 4♡. Looking at the loser situation from the long-trump hand (North), you can see three potential losers in the red suits and a possible fourth loser in clubs. What is your plan?

Suppose you make the obvious plan, winning the opening lead and playing a round of trumps. You intend to play up to the ◇K, and if East proves to have the ◇A, eventually you will take a finesse in clubs. As you can see, if you play the hand this way, ou will go down!

A better plan is to play diamonds by leading towards the jack on the first round, planning to lead towards the king next. Most of the time this will allow you to establish a diamond winner for your tenth trick. Howeve, an alert East will win Trick 2 with the trump ace and switch to the ♣10. Even if you subsequently set up a diamond trick, it will be too late. East will clear the clubs when he wins the ◇Q and the defenders will score the setting trick in clubs when they are in with the ◇A.

You must start work on the diamonds immediately, before drawing trumps. So, win the spade lead with the king and lead a low diamond towards the jack. Luck is immediately with you because East holds the ◇Q. Suppose he rises with the queen and switches to the ♣10. Resist the temptation to try a finesse of the jack! You will go down if you do this (you need the club king as an entry later because East can overruff a third round of spades). Win with the ♣A instead and lead the ◇J, clearing your diamond trick. When East wins and plays another club, try the jack if you like. It is covered by the queen and dummy's ace. You discard your club loser on the established ◇K, both defenders following. Finally you can draw trumps and claim the contract.

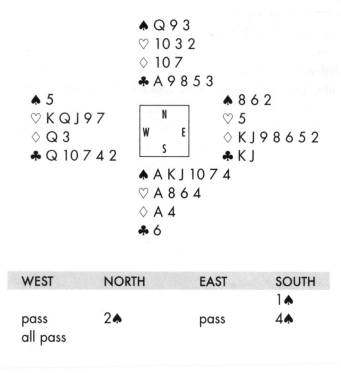

	♠ Q 9 3	
	♡ 10 3 2	
	◇ 10 7	
	♣ A 9 8 5 3	

♠ 5   ♠ 8 6 2
♡ K Q J 9 7 ♡ 5
◇ Q 3   ◇ K J 9 8 6 5 2
♣ Q 10 7 4 2 ♣ K J

	♠ A K J 10 7 4	
	♡ A 8 6 4	
	◇ A 4	
	♣ 6	

WEST	NORTH	EAST	SOUTH
			1♠
pass	2♠	pass	4♠
all pass			

West leads the ♡K against your spade game and you win with the
♡A. What is your plan for ten tricks?

There are four potential losers in the red suits. A 3-3 heart break
would allow you to score the thirteenth heart. Similarly a 2-2 trump
break would allow you to draw trumps and then ruff the fourth round
of hearts. What can be done if neither suit breaks so conveniently?

The solution is to concede two heart tricks without drawing any
trumps. Since you hold all the top trumps, there will be no problem
in ruffing the fourth heart high and subsequently drawing trumps.
Are there any potential traps in this line?

Yes indeed, as the original declarer found out! He won the heart
lead and immediately conceded a heart. East threw the ♣J on this

trick and West promptly cashed another top heart, allowing East to throw his ♣K. When West switched to the ♣Q declarer could not afford to have dummy's ♣A ruffed. He played low from dummy, allowing the ♣Q to win; his intention was to use the ♣A later, to discard his losing diamond.

West found the best continuation of a fourth heart, which was ruffed with the ♠9. Declarer then played the ace and queen of trumps, hoping for a 2-2 break. No, East still had a trump left. He ruffed the ♣A and that was down one.

Did you spot declarer's mistake? To make the game, declarer needed to cash the ♣A before conceding a heart. Nothing could then have prevented him from scoring a heart ruff as his tenth trick.

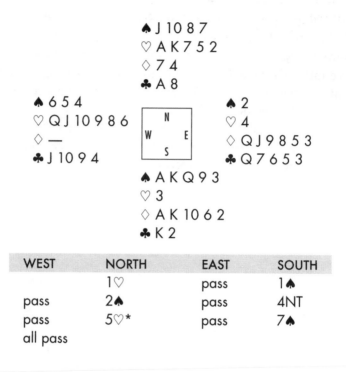

♠ J 10 8 7
♡ A K 7 5 2
◇ 7 4
♣ A 8

♠ 6 5 4
♡ Q J 10 9 8 6
◇ —
♣ J 10 9 4

♠ 2
♡ 4
◇ Q J 9 8 5 3
♣ Q 7 6 5 3

♠ A K Q 9 3
♡ 3
◇ A K 10 6 2
♣ K 2

WEST	NORTH	EAST	SOUTH
	1♡	pass	1♠
pass	2♠	pass	4NT
pass	5♡*	pass	7♠
all pass			

West leads the ♡Q against your grand slam. Looking at the losers in the long-trump hand (South) you see that you must dispose of the three potential losers in the diamond suit. The 'obvious' way to play would be to ruff two diamonds with high trumps in the dummy and throw the remaining diamond loser on dummy's spare heart winner.

This line would work if trumps were 2-2 or if diamonds broke 4-2 or better. However, even lucky players do not get good breaks all the time. Suppose the cards lie as in the diagram. You play two rounds of trumps and East shows out on the second round. When you play the ◇A West pounces gleefully with a trump! Down one.

This is one of the unusual hands where you will fare better if you consider matters from the dummy. Dummy has three potential losers in hearts. If you ruff all of these in the South hand you will make the grand slam without relying on any good breaks.

Ruff a heart with the ♠A at Trick 2. Overtake the ♠9 with the ♠10 and ruff a heart with the ♠K. Return to dummy with the ♣A and ruff the last heart loser with the ♠Q. A low trump to the jack allows you to draw trumps. You score four trump tricks in dummy, three ruffs and three ace-king combinations. That comes to thirteen!

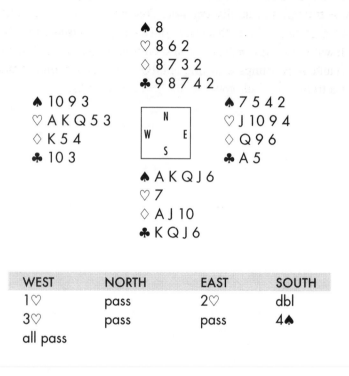

♠ 8
♡ 8 6 2
◇ 8 7 3 2
♣ 9 8 7 4 2

♠ 10 9 3
♡ A K Q 5 3
◇ K 5 4
♣ 10 3

♠ 7 5 4 2
♡ J 10 9 4
◇ Q 9 6
♣ A 5

♠ A K Q J 6
♡ 7
◇ A J 10
♣ K Q J 6

WEST	NORTH	EAST	SOUTH
1♡	pass	2♡	dbl
3♡	pass	pass	4♠
all pass			

The leap to 4♠ may seem a bit macho, but you don't need very much from partner. If he can provide as little as the ◇Q you will be a heavy favorite to make the contract. Alas, even that is beyond him.

West leads two top hearts against your game in spades. Assuming the trumps break 4-3, as you must hope, you have four losers in the South hand — one heart, two diamonds and one club. It is not possible to take two finesses in diamonds because you would need two entries to dummy. The obvious plan is to discard one of the diamond losers on dummy's fifth club.

Suppose, after ruffing the heart lead, you draw trumps in four rounds. That's no good. When you knock out the ♣A you will have no protection in hearts. A better idea is to play on clubs at Trick 3. When East takes the ♣A, on the first or second round, he will return a heart. You cannot afford to ruff, reducing yourself to only three trumps, so you discard a diamond loser from your hand. If East persists with a fourth round of hearts you will now be able to ruff with dummy's ♠8! You can then return to your hand with the ◇A and draw trumps with your A-K-Q-J. If East returns a diamond (or a trump) instead, you will simply draw trumps.

Problem 21

```
            ♠ 9 3 2
            ♡ 6 3
            ◇ 10 8 7 5 3 2
            ♣ 7 6
♡K led
            ♠ A K Q 10 7 6 4
            ♡ A 5 2
            ◇ 4
            ♣ A Q
```

WEST	NORTH	EAST	SOUTH
1♡	pass	1NT	4♠
all pass			

West leads the ♡K against your spade game. What is your plan for ten tricks? (You will find that East holds all three missing trumps.)

Problem 22

```
            ♠ A 9 6
            ♡ 8 7 5
            ◇ 7 5 2
            ♣ A 8 3 2
♡J led
            ♠ K Q 7 4 2
            ♡ A K Q
            ◇ A K 6
            ♣ K 4
```

WEST	NORTH	EAST	SOUTH
			2♣
pass	2NT	pass	3♠
pass	4♣	pass	4◇
pass	4♠	pass	6♠
all pass			

Your slam will be easy if trumps break 3-2. What can be done against a 4-1 spade break?

Problem 23

```
                    ♠ 5 3 2
                    ♡ A 8
                    ◇ 8 5 2
                    ♣ K Q J 8 7
♡K led
                    ♠ A K J 8 7 6 4
                    ♡ 7 5
                    ◇ A Q 3
                    ♣ 4
```

WEST	NORTH	EAST	SOUTH
1♡	pass	pass	4♠
all pass			

West leads the ♡K against your spade game. How will you play?

Problem 24

```
                    ♠ 10 6 2
                    ♡ 7 6 5
                    ◇ A Q 3 2
                    ♣ A 8 5
♣K led
                    ♠ A K Q 4
                    ♡ A K Q 4 3
                    ◇ 4
                    ♣ 9 7 4
```

WEST	NORTH	EAST	SOUTH
			1♡
2NT*	dbl	3◇	3♠
pass	4♣	pass	4NT
pass	5♡*	pass	6♡
all pass			

West, who showed both minors with his Unusual Notrump overcall, leads the ♣K against 6♡. How will you play?

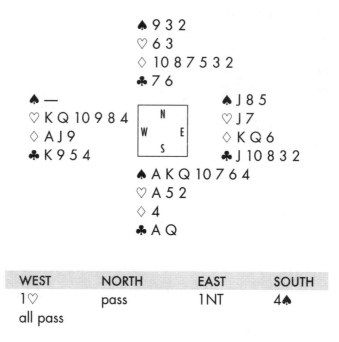

♠ 9 3 2
♡ 6 3
◇ 10 8 7 5 3 2
♣ 7 6

♠ —
♡ K Q 10 9 8 4
◇ A J 9
♣ K 9 5 4

♠ J 8 5
♡ J 7
◇ K Q 6
♣ J 10 8 3 2

♠ A K Q 10 7 6 4
♡ A 5 2
◇ 4
♣ A Q

WEST	NORTH	EAST	SOUTH
1♡	pass	1NT	4♠
all pass			

East-West would have made 5♡ but this was difficult to judge. They let you play in 4♠ and West leads the ♡K. What is your plan?

There are four potential losers in the long-trump hand. Nothing can be done about the diamond loser but in clubs you have the option of a finesse. In hearts you may be able to save a loser by ruffing the third round. Suppose you win the heart lead and play the ace of trumps, discovering that East holds all three trumps. You will not now be able to draw trumps before ruffing a heart in dummy. So, if hearts break 6-2 East will be able to overruff the dummy. What can you do about it?

You must use an unusual technique known as 'trading ruffs'. You aim to swap a risky heart ruff for a safe club ruff. At Trick 3 you lead a second round of hearts. Let's assume that East wins with the jack and switches to a club. You rise with the club ace and lead a third round of hearts. Instead of ruffing this, you discard dummy's last club! Nothing can now prevent you from ruffing the ♣Q in dummy to score a tenth trick. You will lose two hearts and one diamond.

Following this line, you might go down if East held three trumps and three hearts. He would play a trump when he won the second heart and another trump when he won the third heart. For that reason, the very best play is to concede a heart before drawing any trumps!

```
              ♠ A 9 6
              ♡ 8 7 5
              ◇ 7 5 2
              ♣ A 8 3 2
♠ 3                            ♠ J 10 8 5
♡ J 10 9 2      ┌──────┐       ♡ 6 4 3
◇ J 8 4 3       │   N  │       ◇ Q 10 9
♣ Q 10 6 5    W │      │ E     ♣ J 9 7
                │   S  │
                └──────┘
              ♠ K Q 7 4 2
              ♡ A K Q
              ◇ A K 6
              ♣ K 4
```

WEST	NORTH	EAST	SOUTH
			2♣
pass	2NT	pass	3♠
pass	4♣	pass	4◇
pass	4♠	pass	6♠
all pass			

There will be twelve easy tricks if trumps break 3-2. What can be done if trumps break 4-1? Since there is an unavoidable diamond loser it may seem that you cannot survive a loser in the trump suit. Think again! If you can score your seven side-suit winners and three top trumps, you can bring your total to twelve tricks by scoring two of the low trumps in your hand.

You win the heart lead and test the trumps by cashing the king and queen. If the suit breaks 3-2 you will draw the last trump and claim twelve tricks. When the cards lie as in the diagram West will show out on the second trump. You must now aim to ruff two clubs in your hand. Before doing this, it is essential to cash all your winners in the red suits. (Otherwise East might be able to discard in a red suit when you take the club ruffs.) You cash the red winners successfully and continue with the king and ace of clubs, followed by a club ruff.

Now you can see the benefit of leaving the ♠A as a potential entry to dummy. You cross to it and survey this end position:

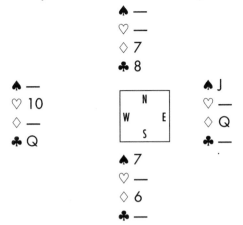

If East was on lead he could draw your last trump and cash the ◇Q. No, the dummy is on lead! 'Play the last club, please,' you say. Whether or not East chooses to ruff with his master trump, your ♠7 will be promoted and you will make the small slam.

What if West had held four trumps? Could you ever make the slam then? It's just possible if he has exactly the right distribution. If West's shape was 4-3-2-4, you would reach this end position:

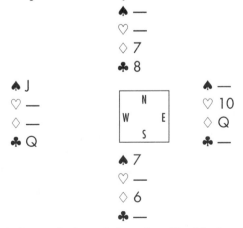

You lead dummy's last club and ruff with the ♠7. West has to follow suit and twelve tricks are in the bag. At Trick 13 West may enjoy the moment as he ruffs his partner's diamond winner!

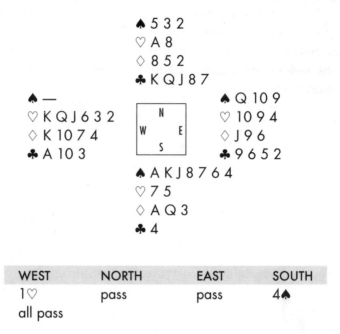

WEST	NORTH	EAST	SOUTH
1♡	pass	pass	4♠
all pass			

You bid 4♠ on your own hand and West leads the ♡K, an annoying lead because it kills a potential entry to dummy's tricks in the club suit. How should you plan the play?

All will be easy if trumps break 2-1. After drawing trumps with the ace and king, you will be able to set up the clubs and reach dummy with the trump five. So, what can be done if trumps break 3-0, in particular with East holding the trump length?

You should win the second round of hearts, thereby ensuring that East cannot gain the lead in the suit. Your next move is to finesse the jack of trumps! When the cards lie as in the diagram, the trump finesse will win and West will show out. Without drawing the remaining trumps, you will then play a club. If West declines to rise with the ace you will have ten tricks. If instead West plays the ace on the first round, he will be endplayed. Another heart would give a ruff-and-discard, a diamond would be into your tenace, and a club would give the lead to dummy's winners in the suit.

What if the spade finesse had lost to the queen with West? Again you would be safe. Trumps would have broken 2-1 in that case and you would have no problem in setting up some winners in clubs and reaching them on the third round of trumps, with dummy's ♠5.

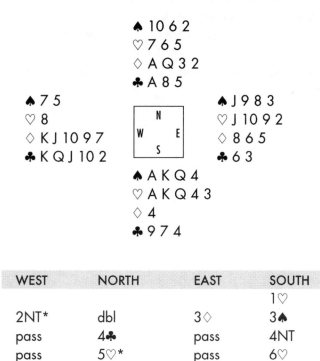

♠ 10 6 2
♡ 7 6 5
◇ A Q 3 2
♣ A 8 5

♠ 7 5
♡ 8
◇ K J 10 9 7
♣ K Q J 10 2

♠ J 9 8 3
♡ J 10 9 2
◇ 8 6 5
♣ 6 3

♠ A K Q 4
♡ A K Q 4 3
◇ 4
♣ 9 7 4

WEST	NORTH	EAST	SOUTH
			1♡
2NT*	dbl	3◇	3♠
pass	4♣	pass	4NT
pass	5♡*	pass	6♡
all pass			

You reach the contract of 6♡ after West has intervened with the Unusual Notrump, showing length in both the minors. West leads the ♣K and when the dummy goes down you see that the bidding has been somewhat ambitious.

You win with the ♣A and play two rounds of trumps, discovering the 4-1 break. What is the loser situation? The potential loser in spades can be ruffed safely in the dummy because the 2NT overcall tells you that East will be long in both the major suits. One of your club losers can be discarded on the second diamond (assuming the finesse is right). But doesn't this still leave you with a trump loser and a seemingly unavoidable loser in the club suit? Not necessarily! You have six winners in the side suits, assuming the diamond finesse is right. If you can score six trump tricks in addition, the total will come to twelve.

You finesse the ◇Q successfully and throw a club loser on the ◇A. After ruffing a diamond in your hand, scoring one of your low trumps, you play the three top spades. West shows out on the third round and you ruff the ♠4 with dummy's last trump. This is the end position that you have reached:

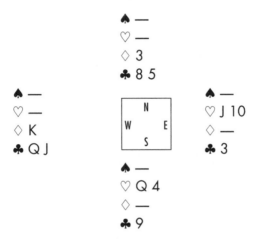

You lead dummy's last diamond and — as if by magic — one of your two losers disappears! If East discards a club you will score your ♡4. The ♡Q will be your twelfth trick and the defenders can scrap over the last trick. If instead East chooses to ruff dummy's last diamond, you will simply discard your club loser and score the last two tricks in trumps. The ♡4 is not worth a trick by right but you promote it into a trick by leading a plain card towards it.

Problem 25

                    ♠ 5 3 2
                    ♡ 2
                    ◇ A Q J 9 7 6 2
                    ♣ 10 4

♠10 led

                    ♠ A K Q J
                    ♡ A 6 4
                    ◇ —
                    ♣ A K 8 7 6 2

WEST	NORTH	EAST	SOUTH
			1♣
pass	1◇	pass	2♠
pass	3◇	pass	3♡
pass	3♠	pass	6♠
all pass			

Yes, 6♣ would have been easier, but what are your prospects here?

Problem 26

                    ♠ 7 6
                    ♡ 9 6 5 3
                    ◇ 8 5 4 3 2
                    ♣ 10 9

♡2 led

                    ♠ A K Q 10 9 5
                    ♡ 10
                    ◇ A Q 9
                    ♣ A K Q

WEST	NORTH	EAST	SOUTH
		1♡	dbl
pass	2◇	pass	2♡
pass	3◇	pass	4♠
all pass			

East wins ♡K and persists with the ♡A. How will you play?

Problem 27

```
              ♠ K
              ♡ J 4 2
              ◇ K 8 7 2
              ♣ J 10 9 6 2
♡7 led
              ♠ 8 7 6
              ♡ A K Q 10 9 8 5
              ◇ A 5
              ♣ A
```

WEST	NORTH	EAST	SOUTH
			1♡
1♠	2♡	4♠	6♡
all pass			

Expecting partner to be short in spades, you leap to 6♡. How will you play the slam on a trump lead, West following suit?

Problem 28 ·

```
              ♠ 10 9 5 3 2
              ♡ Q J 9 6 5
              ◇ A K
              ♣ 7
♣K led
              ♠ A K Q J
              ♡ A K
              ◇ J 8 2
              ♣ Q 9 5 2
```

WEST	NORTH	EAST	SOUTH
			2NT
pass	3♡*	pass	3♠
pass	5♡	pass	6♠
all pass			

West leads the ♣K against 6♠ and switches to a diamond, won in the dummy. When you play a trump, West shows out. What now?

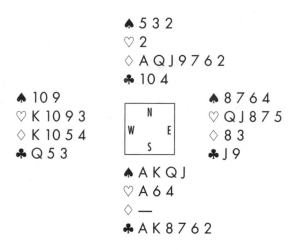

♠ 5 3 2
♡ 2
♢ A Q J 9 7 6 2
♣ 10 4

♠ 10 9
♡ K 10 9 3
♢ K 10 5 4
♣ Q 5 3

♠ 8 7 6 4
♡ Q J 8 7 5
♢ 8 3
♣ J 9

♠ A K Q J
♡ A 6 4
♢ —
♣ A K 8 7 6 2

WEST	NORTH	EAST	SOUTH
			1♣
pass	1♢	pass	2♠
pass	3♢	pass	3♡
pass	3♠	pass	6♠
all pass			

West leads the ♠10, which you win your hand. What are your prospects? You have two potential losers in hearts and one or more in clubs. Both suits offer the potential of a ruff in the dummy and there is one discard available on the ♢A. Let's see first what will happen if your next move is to ruff either a heart or a club.

Suppose you play the ♡A, ruff a heart at Trick 3 and throw your last heart on the ♢A. If you then play the top clubs and take a club ruff, East will refuse to overruff. You will have to ruff a diamond to reach the South hand and will lose trump control. Nor can you concede a round of clubs after discarding the heart. The defenders would then be able to force you in diamonds.

Suppose instead that you start by playing the ♣AK and ruffing a club. That's no good: East will overruff and return a trump, leaving you with two heart losers!

The only winning line is to duck a club trick before drawing trumps — simply play a low club from both hands at Trick 2! No unnecessary risk is involved because you need a 3-2 club break anyway. Whatever the defenders return, you will ruff a heart in dummy and discard a heart on the ◇A. You can then draw trumps and claim.

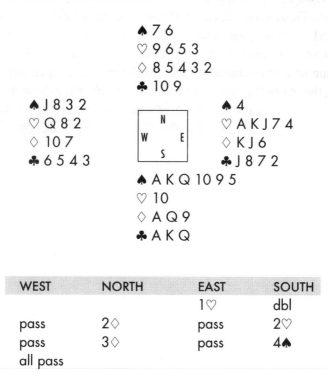

| ♠ 7 6 |
| ♡ 9 6 5 3 |
| ◇ 8 5 4 3 2 |
| ♣ 10 9 |

♠ J 8 3 2   ♠ 4
♡ Q 8 2   ♡ A K J 7 4
◇ 10 7   ◇ K J 6
♣ 6 5 4 3   ♣ J 8 7 2

   ♠ A K Q 10 9 5
   ♡ 10
   ◇ A Q 9
   ♣ A K Q

WEST	NORTH	EAST	SOUTH
		1♡	dbl
pass	2◇	pass	2♡
pass	3◇	pass	4♠
all pass			

West leads the ♡2 against your spade game, East winning with the king and persisting with the heart ace. How will you play the contract?

You have three potential losers in the red suits and one potential loser in trumps if that suit breaks badly. In such contracts you should assume that the main suit will break badly and plan accordingly. Suppose, for example, that you ruff the second heart and play two top trumps, discovering the bad break. You can sit back in your chair for as long as you like but there will be no way to recover!

West's lead of the ♡2 suggests an honor in the suit, the way many players lead. Whether or not that is the case, the fact that East won the first trick with the ♡K suggests that West holds the ♡Q. It follows that East is very likely indeed to hold the ◇K. You should therefore plan to take a diamond finesse. Ruff the second heart and cash the ace and king of clubs. Now ruff the club queen to gain an entry to dummy. You finesse the ◇Q successfully and, only then, test the trump suit. The 4-1 break will now come as a pleasant surprise to you. It means that your play of ruffing a winning club was the only way to make the contract.

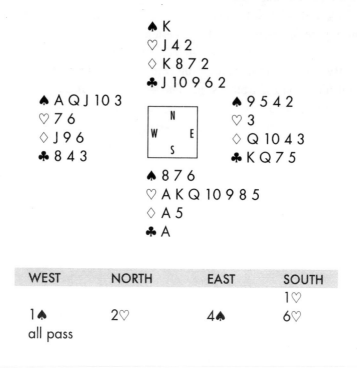

	♠ K	
	♡ J 4 2	
	◇ K 8 7 2	
	♣ J 10 9 6 2	

♠ A Q J 10 3		♠ 9 5 4 2
♡ 7 6	N	♡ 3
◇ J 9 6	W E	◇ Q 10 4 3
♣ 8 4 3	S	♣ K Q 7 5

	♠ 8 7 6	
	♡ A K Q 10 9 8 5	
	◇ A 5	
	♣ A	

WEST	NORTH	EAST	SOUTH
			1♡
1♠	2♡	4♠	6♡
all pass			

Expecting your partner to be short in spades, you impress everyone at the table by leaping to 6♡. All would have been easy if West had led the ♠A but he meanly starts with a trump. What is your plan?

If the defender with the spade ace began with only one trump, you will still be able to take two spade ruffs. It would be a mistake to lead a spade at Trick 2, however, because dummy's club suit offers you an alternative route to twelve tricks. You should cash the ♣A before playing a spade. West wins with the ♠A and, as you feared, plays a second round of trumps. The best chance now is to find East with the king and queen of clubs. (This is more likely than finding West with ♣Kx or ♣Qx, when you could ruff out West's honor and then finesse against East's remaining honor.)

You win the second round of trumps with dummy's jack and lead the ♣J. East covers with the king and you ruff. A diamond to the king returns the lead to dummy and you lead the ♣10. If East covers, you will ruff and return to dummy with a spade ruff to throw your losing diamond on the established ♣9. If instead East plays low, you will discard your diamond loser immediately.

By playing in this fashion you combine two chances, always a good idea. You succeed when the defender with the ♠A cannot play a second trump. You succeed also when East holds both club honors.

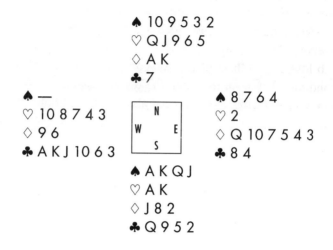

♠ 10 9 5 3 2
♡ Q J 9 6 5
♢ A K
♣ 7

♠ —
♡ 10 8 7 4 3
♢ 9 6
♣ A K J 10 6 3

♠ 8 7 6 4
♡ 2
♢ Q 10 7 5 4 3
♣ 8 4

♠ A K Q J
♡ A K
♢ J 8 2
♣ Q 9 5 2

WEST	NORTH	EAST	SOUTH
			2NT
pass	3♡*	pass	3♠
pass	5♡	pass	6♠
all pass			

North uses a transfer sequence to show two long majors and slam-try values. With six top cards in his suits, you rely on him for sufficient minor-suit controls and bid 6♠. West leads the ♣K, switching to a diamond. You win in the dummy and play a trump, West showing out. What now?

If you look at the losers in the long-trump (North) hand, it may seem that there is just the one loser in clubs, already conceded. Anyone coming to that conclusion will draw trumps in four rounds, unblock the ace and king of hearts and... oh dear! The hearts break 5-1. Down one.

When a contract appears to be cold you must look for any bad break that might beat you. Here a 5-1 heart break would defeat the simple line of drawing trumps first. How can you overcome such a division?

You should consider the losers in the South hand, in effect reversing the 'dummy'. You have one diamond loser there and four club losers. The best plan is to ruff two clubs and discard a diamond and a club on the ♡QJ. After one round of trumps, ruff a club with the ♠10. Return to a trump and ruff a club with the ♠9. Draw trumps, unblock the hearts, cross to a diamond and discard your last two losers on the ♡QJ. Easy!

Problem 29

♠ 9 5 3
♡ A Q
◇ A K Q J 7 6
♣ 9 8

♣K led

♠ K Q J 10 7 2
♡ K 10 4
◇ 10 4
♣ 6 2

WEST	NORTH	EAST	SOUTH
			2♠*
pass	4♠	all pass	

Your weak two is raised to game and West leads the ♣K. East overtakes with the ♣A and switches to the ◇2. How will you play?

Problem 30

♠ A Q 4
♡ 10 7 5
◇ A 5 4
♣ K Q 7 2

♡K led

♠ K J 8 2
♡ 3
◇ K 9 3 2
♣ A J 9 4

WEST	NORTH	EAST	SOUTH
1♡	dbl	3♡	4♠
all pass			

You arrive in 4♠ on a 4-3 fit and West leads the ♡K followed by the ♡A. How will you the play the contract?

Problem 31

```
              ♠ J 10
              ♡ A 7 6
              ◇ A Q 7
              ♣ A 8 7 6 4
♣J led
              ♠ K Q 6 4 2
              ♡ K Q J 9 3
              ◇ K
              ♣ Q 2
```

WEST	NORTH	EAST	SOUTH
	1NT	pass	2♡*
pass	2♠	pass	3♡
pass	4♡	pass	4NT
pass	5♣*	pass	6♡
all pass			

West leads the ♣J against your slam. How will you plan the play?

Problem 32

```
              ♠ A K 8 2
              ♡ 6
              ◇ A K 6 3 2
              ♣ A 5 2
♣K led
              ♠ 7 4
              ♡ A Q 10 9 8 3
              ◇ 9 5
              ♣ 9 8 3
```

WEST	NORTH	EAST	SOUTH
			2♡*
pass	4♡	all pass	

West leads the ♣K against your heart game. How will you play?

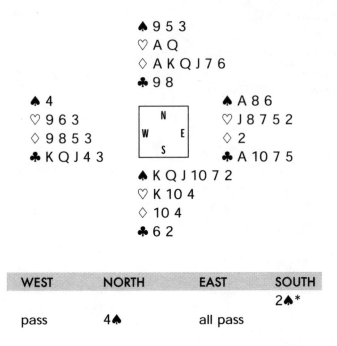

WEST	NORTH	EAST	SOUTH
			2♠*
pass	4♠	all pass	

Your weak two in spades is raised to game and West leads the ♣K. The defense now takes an unexpected turn. East overtakes with the ♣A and switches to the ◇2. How do you read the situation now?

The odds are high that East has a singleton diamond and probably the ace of trumps too. His plan is to win the first round of trumps and then cross to his partner's hand in clubs to receive a diamond ruff. Assuming that the cards do lie in this fashion, what can you do about it?

If you play a trump at Trick 3 you can see from the diagram that you will go down, suffering a diamond ruff. To avoid the ruff you must perform a very unusual maneuver. After winning the diamond switch, you play the ace of hearts and then overtake the queen of hearts with the king. Next you lead the ten of hearts.

Luck is with you when West plays low. You throw dummy's remaining club and East (the safe hand) has to win the trick. East will probably play a fourth round of hearts now, in case he can promote a trump trick for his partner. You discard your last club and ruff in dummy. When you draw trumps, you find that East does indeed hold the ace of the suit. No defensive ruff is possible, and the contract is yours. The clever move in hearts is known as a **Scissors Coup** because it cuts the defenders' communications.

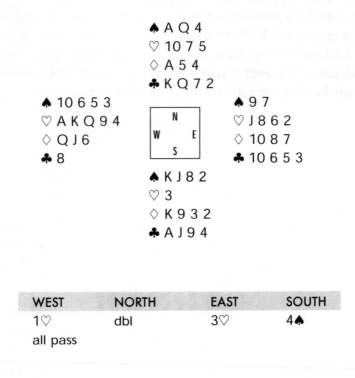

WEST	NORTH	EAST	SOUTH
1♡	dbl	3♡	4♠
all pass			

You arrive in 4♠ on a 4-3 fit and West leads two top hearts. How should you the play the contract?

Suppose you ruff the second round of hearts and draw three rounds of trumps. If the trump suit breaks 3-3 you will have a lucky escape, making your game. In the more likely event that trumps break 4-2, as in the diagram, you will fall well short of your target. West will ruff the second round of clubs and cash his remaining hearts.

On deals such as this, there is a standard way of maintaining trump control. You refuse to ruff in the long-trump hand and wait until you can ruff in the short-trump hand. How does that work here?

You discard a diamond from your hand on the second and third round of hearts. If West now switches elsewhere, you will win and draw trumps in four rounds, claiming the rest of the tricks. If instead West perseveres with a fourth round of hearts, you will ruff with dummy's ♠4. East's double raise in hearts suggests that he will follow to the fourth round of hearts. Should he in fact over-ruff, you will overruff in your own hand and still make the contract unless East has overruffed from a doubleton trump.

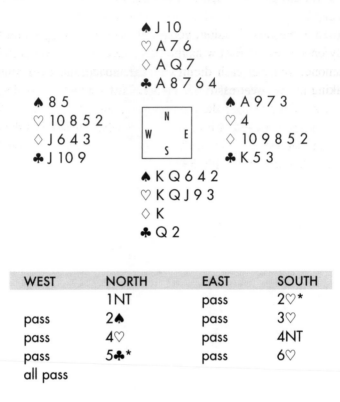

♠ J 10
♡ A 7 6
◇ A Q 7
♣ A 8 7 6 4

♠ 8 5
♡ 10 8 5 2
◇ J 6 4 3
♣ J 10 9

♠ A 9 7 3
♡ 4
◇ 10 9 8 5 2
♣ K 5 3

♠ K Q 6 4 2
♡ K Q J 9 3
◇ K
♣ Q 2

WEST	NORTH	EAST	SOUTH
	1NT	pass	2♡*
pass	2♠	pass	3♡
pass	4♡	pass	4NT
pass	5♣*	pass	6♡
all pass			

Your 3♡ promises five hearts (with 5-4 shape you would have started with Stayman). North shows three aces with his 1430 response to Roman Keycard Blackwood.

You win the ♣J lead with the ♣A and cash the ace and queen of diamonds, throwing your club loser. (You cannot afford to use the ♡A to untangle three tricks in diamonds.) What now? Suppose you play the king and ace of trumps, finding a 4-1 trump break. You cannot draw trumps before playing spades because East would then win the first spade (leaving the suit blocked) and force your last trump with a third round of diamonds. If instead you play spades while West still holds two trumps, East will win the second spade and give his partner a spade ruff with the ♡8 ahead of dummy's ♡7.

To avoid this situation, you must cash just the ♡K and then play on spades. If East wins the first spade and forces you with a diamond, you can cash dummy's other spade and draw trumps, making the contract easily. If instead East wins the second spade and plays a third spade, the ♡A remains in dummy to overruff West if necessary. The only tricky situation is when West holds the ♠A, wins the second round of spades and plays a third round. Your best chance then is to ruff with the ♡A.

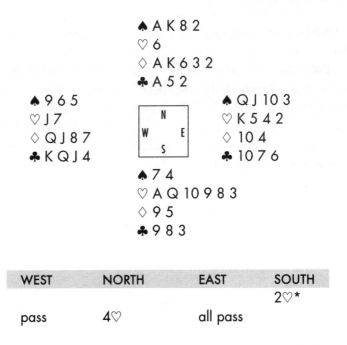

	♠ A K 8 2	
	♡ 6	
	◇ A K 6 3 2	
	♣ A 5 2	
♠ 9 6 5		♠ Q J 10 3
♡ J 7		♡ K 5 4 2
◇ Q J 8 7		◇ 10 4
♣ K Q J 4		♣ 10 7 6
	♠ 7 4	
	♡ A Q 10 9 8 3	
	◇ 9 5	
	♣ 9 8 3	

WEST	NORTH	EAST	SOUTH
			2♡*
pass	4♡	all pass	

West leads the ♣K against your heart game and you win in the dummy. (You might choose to win the second round instead but it makes little difference). If you can escape for one trump loser you will make the game easily. What is the best play in trumps, aiming solely for this target? When the suit breaks 3-3, it is an even-money gamble whether you finesse the ten or the queen. When East has a doubleton, it does not matter which finesse you take — his honor will fall on the second round anyway. When West has a doubleton trump, there is a big advantage to finessing the queen rather than the ten. Finessing the queen restricts your losers to one when West holds Jx. Finessing the ten does not restrict your losers to one when West holds Kx. So, your next move should be to finesse the ♡Q.

When the cards lie as in the diagram, the finesse will succeed and the ♡J will fall from West under your ace. You will drive out the ♡K with the ♡10 and soon have ten tricks.

Suppose next that both defenders had followed with a low heart on the second round. What would be the best continuation then?

Playing a third heart would succeed only when hearts were 3-3. A better idea is to play ace, king and another diamond, aiming to set up a club discard. You will succeed when diamonds are 3-3, when East has two diamonds (if he ruffs the third or fourth diamond, you will throw a club), or when East is 4-4 in the red suits. Playing a third trump is around a 47% line. Playing on diamonds instead gives you a 70% chance.

Problem 33

```
            ♠ 10 7 3
            ♡ 9 7 2
            ◇ A Q J 7 6
            ♣ A 5
♡10 led
            ♠ A K 9 8 6 4
            ♡ J 5 3
            ◇ K 8 5
            ♣ Q
```

WEST	NORTH	EAST	SOUTH
			1♠
pass	2◇	2♡	2♠
pass	4♠	all pass	

East cashes three rounds of hearts, West throwing the ♣2 on the third round. East switches to the ◇4. How will you play?

Problem 34

```
            ♠ Q 10 8
            ♡ A 9 2
            ◇ A J 6 5 2
            ♣ A 9
♠2 led
            ♠ A K J 5 4
            ♡ K Q J 8 6
            ◇ 4
            ♣ 8 7
```

WEST	NORTH	EAST	SOUTH
			1♠
pass	2◇	pass	2♡
pass	3♠	pass	4NT
pass	5♣*	pass	5◇*
pass	6♠*	pass	7♠
all pass			

How will you play this grand slam on a trump lead?

Problem 35

```
            ♠ Q J 10 7 4
            ♡ A
            ◇ A Q 8 5
            ♣ Q 5 2
♠2 led
            ♠ A K 9 5
            ♡ J 3
            ◇ 7 6 4
            ♣ A K J 7
```

WEST	NORTH	EAST	SOUTH
			1NT
pass	2♡*	pass	3♠*
pass	4NT	pass	5♣*
pass	6♠	all pass	

West leads the ♠2 against your spade slam. How will you play the contract? (You will find that trumps are 2-2.)

Problem 36

```
            ♠ J 9 3
            ♡ Q J 10 2
            ◇ 8 6 3 2
            ♣ 4 2
♣J led
            ♠ A K Q 10 8 5 4
            ♡ —
            ◇ A K J 5
            ♣ A K
```

WEST	NORTH	EAST	SOUTH
			2♣
pass	2◇	pass	2♠
pass	4♠	pass	6♠
all pass			

How will you attempt to safeguard twelve tricks when West leads the ♣J? (You will find that trumps break 2-1.)

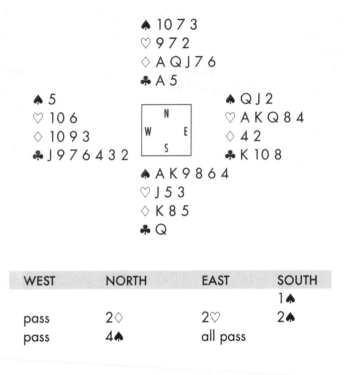

♠ 10 7 3
♡ 9 7 2
◇ A Q J 7 6
♣ A 5

♠ 5
♡ 10 6
◇ 10 9 3
♣ J 9 7 6 4 3 2

♠ Q J 2
♡ A K Q 8 4
◇ 4 2
♣ K 10 8

♠ A K 9 8 6 4
♡ J 5 3
◇ K 8 5
♣ Q

WEST	NORTH	EAST	SOUTH
			1♠
pass	2◇	2♡	2♠
pass	4♠	all pass	

West leads the ♡10 against your spade game and East cashes three rounds of the suit, West discarding the ♣2 on the third round. East switches to the ◇4. How will you play the contract?

You have winners to spare in the side suits and all will depend on picking up the trump suit without loss. The normal play with this holding is to play the ace first, continuing with the king unless an honor falls from West. Do you see any reason to play differently?

You should ask yourself: 'Why on earth did East not play a fourth round of hearts?' That defense would promote a setting trick for the defenders even if their trumps were ♠Jx opposite ♠Qx. Unless East shows some signs of being half asleep, you should assume that he had a good reason for his defense. In other words you should place him with the queen and jack of trumps. Suppose East had played a fourth round of hearts when the cards lie as in the diagram. You would have been forced to play East for the ♠QJ. You would have ruffed with dummy's ♠10 and taken a deep finesse in trumps.

So, win the diamond switch in dummy and finesse the ♠9! If East was asleep all along and the finesse loses to West's ♠Jx or singleton ♠J, console yourself that they could have beaten the contract anyway.

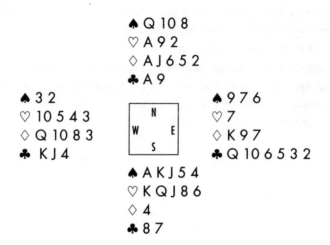

♠ Q 10 8
♡ A 9 2
◇ A J 6 5 2
♣ A 9

♠ 3 2
♡ 10 5 4 3
◇ Q 10 8 3
♣ K J 4

♠ 9 7 6
♡ 7
◇ K 9 7
♣ Q 10 6 5 3 2

♠ A K J 5 4
♡ K Q J 8 6
◇ 4
♣ 8 7

WEST	NORTH	EAST	SOUTH
			1♠
pass	2◇	pass	2♡
pass	3♠	pass	4NT
pass	5♣*	pass	5◇*
pass	6♠*	pass	7♠
all pass			

North's 3♠ was forcing, and you decide to use Roman Keycard Blackwood. When partner shows three aces and the ♠Q you bid a grand slam in spades. How will you play this contract when West leads a low trump?

To dispose of the club loser you must set up dummy's diamond suit. Unless the ◇K and ◇Q fall in three rounds, this will require three ruffs in the South hand. So, you will need a 3-2 trump break, enabling you to draw trumps with dummy's three-card holding.

Win the trump lead with the jack, cross to the ◇A and ruff a diamond low. Play a trump to the 10 and ruff a diamond with the king. Cross to the ♡A and ruff a fourth round of diamonds with the bare ace. Then you can cross to the ♣A and draw East's last trump with dummy's queen. You win the last five tricks with the thirteenth diamond and four top hearts.

Does anything occur to you about the deal? It's a well-established axiom that you should lead a trump against a grand slam but... if West had led a heart or a club, he would have destroyed a vital entry. You would not then have been able to make the contract!

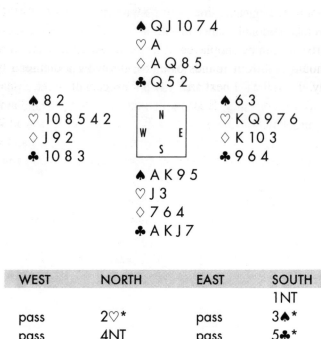

WEST	NORTH	EAST	SOUTH
			1NT
pass	2♡*	pass	3♠*
pass	4NT	pass	5♣*
pass	6♠	all pass	

You break partner's transfer response and show three keycards in response to Roman Keycard Blackwood. How will you play 6♠ when West leads a trump and trumps prove to be 2-2?

It is natural to look for an elimination play. After drawing trumps, the original declarer cashed dummy's ♡A, crossed to the ♣A and ruffed his last heart in dummy. He then played the three remaining club winners and led a low diamond from the South hand. If West had been asleep and played the ◇2, declarer could have inserted the ◇8 to leave East endplayed. However, West was distressingly awake and inserted a mean ◊9. Declarer then had no way to make the contract.

On deals of this sort you should not stop planning as soon as you spot one reasonable line. Look for a way to improve it! Here there is an additional chance that East will hold the king and queen of hearts and can be endplayed in that suit. After drawing trumps, you should cash four rounds of clubs, throwing a diamond from dummy. Lead the ♡J next and, when West cannot cover, discard a diamond from dummy. East wins and must either play a diamond into dummy's ace-queen or give a ruff-and-discard. If instead West does cover the ♡J, ruff in the dummy and return to your hand with a third round of trumps. The original elimination play in diamonds remains intact.

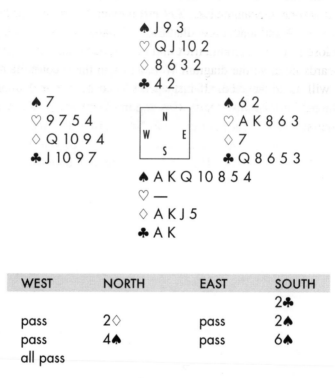

WEST	NORTH	EAST	SOUTH
			2♣
pass	2♦	pass	2♠
pass	4♠	pass	6♠
all pass			

For once (it took you the whole book to manage it!) you bid cautiously. Resisting with some difficulty the temptation to bid a grand slam, you settle for the six-level and West leads the ♣J. How will you give your modest contract of 6♠ the best chance?

There are two potential diamond losers, so you must think what can be done if West holds four or five diamonds to the queen. The best idea is to make use of dummy's hearts. Win the club lead, draw one round of trumps with the ace and cash the other top club. Then cross to dummy with the ♠J and lead the ♡Q. If East does not cover, discard the ◊5 from your hand. West will win the trick and will be endplayed. A diamond return would be into your tenace. A heart return would set up a winner in dummy and a club return would give you a ruff-and-discard. As the cards lie, East will cover the ♡Q with the ♡A. What now?

It is time to change tack. You ruff the heart trick in your hand, cash the ◊A and lead a low diamond. If diamonds break 3-2, you will lose just one diamond trick and make your slam easily. When the cards lie as in the diagram West will win the second diamond and will be end-played. If instead East had held four diamonds, you would ruff his low heart exit and cross to dummy with a trump to finesse the ◊J.

AFTERWORD

What was the main message of this book? It was, of course, that you should always make a plan before embarking on the play of any contrac. If the contract appears to be a certainty, look in good time for any bad break that might defeat you. If instea you or your partner has overbid and there seems to be no hope, seek a distribution of the defenders' cards that might allow you to sneak home.

Some players seem to attend a bridge game with one main objective — to get home as soon as possible! If an opponent pauses for thought, perhaps to plan the play, they give small shake of the head and maybe even consult a wristwatch. These players will never be winners. Bridge is like life, in that you get out of it what you put in. Bridge is not an easy game; indeed, at times it can be downright difficult. To do well, you must try your very best on every hand. We hope you enjoyed the book and wish you the very best of luck next time you venture to the table.

THE 'TEST YOUR BRIDGE TECHNIQUE' SERIES

Elimination Plays
Planning in Suit Contracts
The Simple Squeeze
Entry Management
Planning in Notrump Contracts
Endplays and Coups
Planning the Defense (Suit Contracts)
Planning the Defense (Notrump Contracts)
Safety Plays
Reading the Cards

Master Point Press
416-781-0351
www.masterpointpress.com
Email: info@masterpointpress.com